DEVON LIBRARY & INFORMATION SERVICES
e return this book   or before
k loans

C000311691

Industrial Railways of the South West

Michael Messenger

TWELVEHEADS PRESS

TRURO   2005

All rights reserved. No part of this publication may be reproduced or transmitted in any form or by any means without the prior permission of the publisher.
© Michael Messenger 2005.

TWELVEHEADS PRESS

First published 2005 by Twelveheads Press
ISBN 0 906294 592
British Library Cataloguing-in-Publication Data.
A catalogue record for this book is available from the British Library.
Designed by Alan Kittridge
Printed by The Amadeus Press, Cleckheaton, West Yorkshire.

Contents

FRONT COVER: A Ruston diesel draws loaded ore wagons from beneath the headgear of New Cooks Kitchen Shaft at South Crofty Mine. October 1963

OPPOSITE: *Alfred* at Par Harbour, taking water outside the engine shed. The white clay dust renders the scene dazzling on a sunny day. September 1964

BACK COVER: Exeter Gas Works' Peckett of 1946 shunting at the works. April 1962

Introduction

The industrial railway is the precursor, the ancestor, of the modern railway. More than two centuries before George Stephenson was promoting the inter-city passenger concept the humble industrial railway was at work. From the mines of eastern Europe in the sixteenth century the idea filtered westwards until by the eighteenth century it was well established in many parts of Britain.

But whilst the likes of the Stephensons, Brunel and a string of civil and locomotive engineers spent the nineteenth century taking the main line railway to new heights, the industrial line plodded on, doing the job it was originally conceived for, pausing occasionally to pick up good ideas from its affluent bigger brother, such as steam locomotives and steel rails.

In the south west most industrial lines were as a result of the mineral wealth of the area; mining for tin, copper, lead; quarrying for granite, elvan, slate and several types of clay. Mining and quarrying were the foremost industries using internal railways but were soon joined by heavy engineering and construction works. As industry developed the idea spread and with the growth of

OPPOSITE: South Crofty's 24-inch line running from Robinson's Shaft, in background towards the mill. 1968

main line railways many enterprises had their own links for the transfer of products.

Most lines were devoted to the one industry, and often served just one function within that industry. Many were very short, extremely short, while some places had very extensive systems. South Caradon Mine had nearly 3½ miles of railways underground in its copper workings in the latter half of the nineteenth century, and English China Clays, in 1922, boasted 31 miles of track throughout its many clay pits and brickworks.

The nineteenth and early twentieth centuries were the heyday of the industrial railway, and the end of the latter century saw the use of rail decline dramatically, for all purposes. The old industries closed and industrial railways proved susceptible to rubber tyred competition and to conveyor belts. A few still remain but most are just a memory, some not even leaving enough for an industrial archaeological survey.

Tramroads, tramways, plateways and railways

Many railways terms are ill-defined and often misused. This explanation will try to be helpful rather than presuming to be definitive.

In its simplest definition a railway is a guided trackway whereby vehicles are held on the track by some means, usually a flange. A 'railway' is now accepted as a track with two parallel rails, edge rails, on which run flanged wheels; our modern railway system. The word railway embraces all forms of railway although it is also used as this more precise definition.

A 'plateway' is a railway with flanged L-shaped rails and flangeless wheels, such as the Portreath Tram Road and the Middlebere Plateway. This was an aberration in the evolution of railways, specifically invented about 1800 and which proved an almost total dead end. In the nineteenth century 'tramroad' was used, often in abuse, to describe any primitive railway, whether of plate or edge rails. The tendency today is to limit its use to plateways.

'Tramway' was similarly used - it was the Ordnance Survey's choice of description of almost anything that was not a main line railway. Today it is used for primitive edge railways. An electric street tramway is an entirely different thing, of course.

To complicate matters some early public railways, like the Redruth & Chasewater Railway and the Liskeard & Caradon Railway were really no better than tramways, but they were incorporated by Act of Parliament that named them and stated that they were, legally, railways.

Railroad was used in the very early days of British railways but is now predominant across the Atlantic, where we shall leave it.

In summary, plateways and tramroads have plate rails while tramways and railways have edge rails, in this book at least. The difference between the latter pair depends on how much sophistication the reader attributes to them.

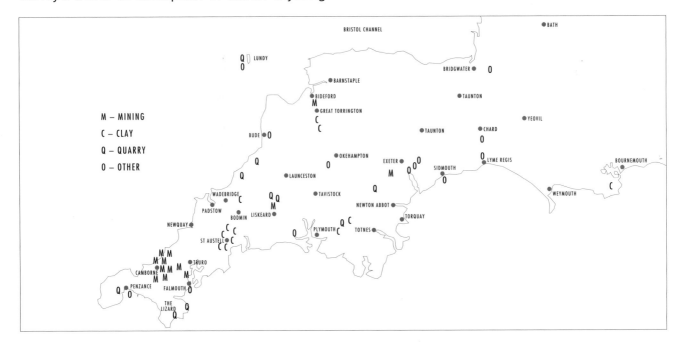

Gauges

Whilst 4ft 8½ins became the standard gauge for Britain and much of the world, plus Brunel's seven foot broad gauge for a time in the south west, industrial railways had no inhibitions, unless linked to a main line. Underground, due to obvious restrictions, gauges were narrow but on surface they were usually much wider; about four feet was initially common. As times progressed gauges narrowed, the economies of construction costs outweighed the lesser load carrying ability. Three feet was popular in the 1870s but the development of 'off-the-shelf' systems in the 1880s and 1890s by Robert Hudson and others brought two foot gauge to the fore and this gauge, or variations like 60cm, became the most popular, especially for mining and quarrying. This is, of course, a generalisation and there were many exceptions but overall much of the south west followed this pattern.

Motive power

Initially, particularly underground, the power source was man and, where appropriate, gravity. Later, on surface, horse and pony power was used. Horses were only rarely used underground; at Levant in the nineteenth century and later at East Pool and Polhigey. Steam power became more common as the nineteenth century progressed. Many lines, due to gradients, were cable operated and a variety of engines, beam and horizontal, powered these.

An interesting feature of many lines was the inclined plane. Useful where a severe change of level was needed, some were powered while others could rely on gravity with descending loaded wagons hauling up empty ones on a parallel line. Although quickly phased out on main line railways they survived on industrial lines until quite recent times.

As the twentieth century developed the internal combustion engine appeared, first in immense stationary engines and then in compact locomotives, such as Ruston & Hornsby developed in the 1930s. Electric power has been limited to battery powered locomotives underground and to stationary haulage engines on surface.

Apart from Bickle of Plymouth, who built a solitary steam engine for use underground in Levant Mine, the only industrial locomotive manufacturer in the south west was Sara & Burgess of Penryn, who built several vertical boiler locomotives for use in Cornwall and Devon.

The Photographs

Most photographs are of my own taking, mainly from the 1960s when many industrial railways were still working, or at least had some interesting remains. I have supplemented them with a few historic photographs from my collection.

The range of subjects, therefore, is restricted to what I saw and photographed. It cannot be, and does not try to be, a comprehensive view but it does, I believe, give a good overall view of the industrial railways of the south west.

Nor is a comprehensive history attempted. Many lines lived and died in great obscurity; they were to their operators simply the necessary machinery of the works, and very few records were made, let alone survived. Histories have to be compiled from all sorts of clues and this is not always possible.

Mining

With a wealth of mineral deposits mining was for many centuries the premier industry in the south west. Although railways first appeared in the early sixteenth century in the mines of eastern Europe, it was a long time before they reached Devon and Cornwall. The first recorded was in 1783 at Happy Union Tin Works, near Pentewan, but a spate of new lines in the 1820s in mines controlled by John Taylor suggests it was he who seriously introduced them into the two western counties.

On the surface the Portreath Tram Road was constructed by John Williams of Scorrier in 1809/12; this was a plateway with flanged rails. The first true railway, with edge rails, in the south west was the Redruth & Chasewater Railway. Although a public railway, authorised by Act, it was entirely owned by John Taylor and opened in 1825 to carry the produce of his mines to Devoran for shipping.

Throughout Cornwall, Devon and west Somerset there have been literally thousands of metal mines, seeking a multitude of minerals; copper, tin, lead, zinc, silver, wolfram and uranium, to name but the principal minerals. All in the last two centuries

OPPOSITE: South Crofty was the last working tin mine in Cornwall and had one of the last working narrow gauge railways. Here a small Ruston waits to take its load to the mill from Robinson's Shaft. 1968

would have had at least a few yards of track for a railway system was considered essential to convey heavy ore, either in the restricted passages underground or on surface between shaft and dressing floor. The extent of South Caradon's network has been noted but another mine nearby was thought, in the 1860s, to be somewhat antiquated with no surface tramways.

Metal mining is one area where rail transport has reigned supreme although, alas, the south west at the time of writing no longer has a single working metal mine.

0-4-0WT Koppel at Basset Mines, Carnkie, Cornwall

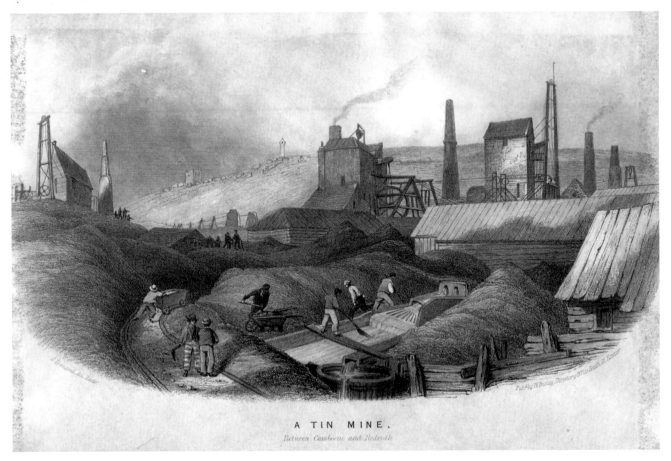

A TIN MINE.
Between Camborne and Redruth

Dolcoath Mine, Camborne, Cornwall
SW 654399/660404 Gauge 1ft 10in

This engraving of Dolcoath Mine was published in 1831 and is one of the oldest known illustrations of a Cornish industrial railway. In the centre men are working a square buddle, to concentrate the tin ore, and to their left can be clearly seen a wagon being wheeled away on a tramway. The perspective is a little peculiar and the wagon seems too narrow for the gauge, but there is no doubt it is an industrial railway. Carn Brea Castle and the Basset monument on the ridge of Carn Brea behind confirms the location. Dolcoath was one of Cornwall's leading copper mines working from before 1758 until 1929. An account of 1827 describes tramways of 9½ inch and 34½ inch gauges on surface. In the 1900s the system was complex enough to warrant two 0-4-2 tank locomotives by Kerr Stuart. Their gauge was 22 inches.

Wheal Jane, near Truro, Cornwall

SW 772427 Gauge 2ft

Not all mine installations were large and extensive, and this photograph of a horse drawing a tram of ore from a small orebin and shaft typifies many of the smaller arrangements. Wheal Jane goes back to 1740 but was re-opened in the period 1905 to 1915 by Falmouth Consols Mines Ltd, when this view of Tremayne Shaft dates from.

A major effort was made to reopen Wheal Jane in 1968 when an extensive 60cm gauge system was installed underground, but little was on surface.

TREMAYNE SHAFT, FALMOUTH CONSOLIDATED LTD. NO. 4

Nangiles Mines, Twelveheads, Cornwall

SW 764420 Gauge 19in

As part of the Wheal Jane re-opening old workings at Nangiles, above Twelveheads village, were made accessible and this remarkable find was made in 1969 in the old stopes at the foot of Crane shaft, not far below the surface. A woodway with rails of three-inch square timbers, with wrought iron strap rails on the bearing surfaces, at a gauge of 19 inches ran through the workings. Wheal Jane always suffered with acid water so this may have been the reason for using wood, or may simply have been more economical at the time. It is thought to date from about 1830.

Portreath Tram Road, Cornwall
Plateway, gauge 3ft 6in

Now preserved in the Royal Cornwall Museum in Truro, but seen here in 1964 at its earlier home in Holman's Museum in Camborne, is what is described as the directors' chaldron. It is probably the world's oldest surviving rail passenger vehicle and was found in a barn near Scorrier about 1930. The plateway was built in 1809/12 from Portreath inland to copper mines near Scorrier and St Day and was all but disued by the 1860s. Much of its route now forms part of the Mineral Tramways Trail.

Redruth & Chasewater Railway, Cornwall
Gauge 4ft

This was Cornwall's first true railway, authorised by Act of Parliament, opened in 1826. It was built by John Taylor to 4 foot gauge to take the produce of his mines near Redruth to the sea at Devoran. Originally horse-drawn, it was rebuilt and steam locomotives introduced in 1854. Here *Miner*, built by Neilson in Glasgow in 1854 as an 0-4-0ST, is at the water tank at Ting Tang Mine, near Carharrack. *Miner* was rebuilt as an 0-6-0ST in 1869, and lasted until the closure of the railway in 1917 when it was probably the last working locomotive in Britain with a domed haycock firebox.

A train of granite from Cheesewring Quarry leaves the site of South Caradon Mine hauled by *Caradon* of 1862. About 1906

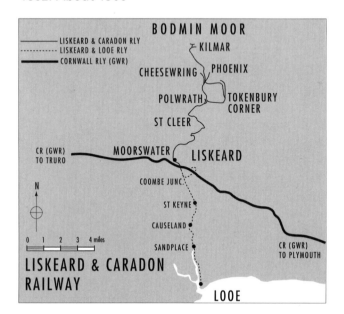

Liskeard & Caradon Railway, Cornwall
Gauge 4ft 8½in

A fascinating railway in the east of Cornwall, this line was built to take the copper ore of the great South Caradon and West Caradon mines, and the granite from Cheesewring Quarry, to the head of the Liskeard & Looe Union Canal at Moorswater. A later line extended down to Looe alongside the canal. For many years the downhill traffic ran by gravity with horses, and later steam, hauling the empties back up the hill the following morning. It opened partially in 1844 from the north and reached Moorswater in 1846. The mines closed in the 1880s and 1890s but the railway struggled on until 1917. The various routes around Caradon Hill and to the north now make superb walks across and into Bodmin Moor.

At South Caradon Mine a mine road crossed the tramway linking Rules and Kittows shafts with the dressing floors. The line of the rails in the cobbles can still be seen, 120 years on.

Basset Mines, Carnkie, Cornwall
SW 680374
A tramway was necessary at this extensive mine to take the tin ores to the ore-stamps and dressing floors. In 1909 a small 0-4-0WT by Orenstein & Koppel of Germany was bought for the tramway. The mine closed in 1918 and the locomotive was sold.

South Crofty Mine, Pool, Cornwall
Gauge 2ft

Parts of South Crofty dated back to the mid-eighteenth century but saw much re-investment in the early 1900s. A lengthy two-foot gauge tramway pre-dated this development and connected several shafts with the mill. To the east were Palmer's and Robinson's (SW 668413) shafts, until the former collapsed in the 1930s, and in the west New Cook's Kitchen shaft (SW 664409), sunk in 1907. Originally horse drawn, diesel locomotives were introduced in the 1950s, and the system closed in 1970, replaced by conveyors.

In 1964 a Ruston Hornsby diesel waits near Robinson's Shaft.

Looking along the tramway towards Cook's Kitchen Shaft. 1968.

OPPOSITE At Robinson's Shaft. The engine shed is the small building in the centre of the picture. Beyond the ore-bins is the engine house with the 80-inch Cornish beam engine. 1968

Battery locomotives of 22 inch gauge were used underground but brought to the surface for charging. Here at Robinson's Shaft no less than nineteen are lined up. The trucks in the foreground are on an isolated length of track servicing a timber preserving tank. Robinson's engine house still is home to a preserved 80-inch (cylinder diameter) Cornish engine of 1854. April 1988

OPPOSITE: Rolling stock at South Croft included the unusual explosive wagons and typical underground U-tip wagon built by Hudson, seen here on surface. 1964

The Brunton Calciners, for separating arsenic from the tin ore, had their own 15-inch gauge tramway, which the writer partially lifted for use in an abortive restoration project. The side tipping wagon, which is now displayed at King Edward Mine, was small enough to be transported in a Morris 1000 Traveller!

Camborne & Redruth Tramway, Cornwall

Essentially an electric street tramway of 3 foot 6 inch gauge between the two towns of its title, the line uniquely also carried minerals from 1904 until 1927 for East Pool & Agar Mine. Two electric locomotives were used and, apart from the mineral branches, the trains ran down the centre of the main road.

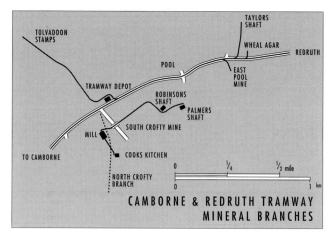

CAMBORNE & REDRUTH TRAMWAY
MINERAL BRANCHES

As late as 1973 sleepers of the former branch to Tolvaddon stamps were still visible beside Tolvaddon Road, just north of its junction with the former A30.

Camborne Tin Ltd, near Camborne, Cornwall
SW 647385 Gauge 60cm
Wheal Pendarves was one of the new tin mines sunk in great optimism in 1968. A 60cm system was installed.

Blue Hills Mine, Cornwall
SW 728516
Although long abandoned Blue Hills was one of those places where odd remains survived. These two wagons, typical of underground use, lay there for many years; the right hand one is made of timber and of 13-inch gauge, the other iron and 18-inch. The nearby waterwheel and stamps have since been restored. April 1964

Cligga Head Mine, Cornwall
SW 681474 Gauge 2ft
Also known as Sally Bottoms, this mine was a war-time reworking for wolfram (an ore of tungsten). Much equipment survived underground including the 24-inch gauge track in the adit at the 300-foot level. This wagon probably dates from an earlier working. November 1969

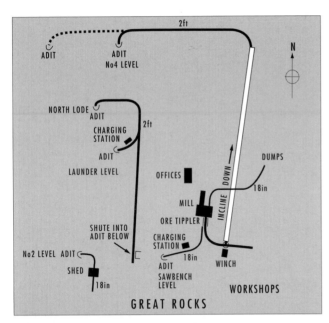

GREAT ROCKS

Ferrubron Manufacturing Co Ltd, Hennock, Devon
SX 828816 Gauges 2ft & 18in

From 1902 to 1969 Great Rock Mine was the source of micaceous iron ore, also known as flaky ore, used in the manufacture of specialised rustproofing paints. It appeared disused when I reached the site but as it was a very wet mines, it only saw use in the dry season. There was plenty to see, with two gauges at Ferrubron, inclines and two homemade battery electric locomotives, named *Golden Arrow* and *Red Arrow*.

The 2ft gauge battery loco *Red Arrow* at its charging station just outside Launder Level. This is probably one of the most rudimentary engine sheds I have seen. August 1968

Golden Arrow lies outside Sawbench Level. August 1968

Bideford Black Pigments Ltd, Bideford, Devon
SS 472263 Gauges 2ft & 18in
A surprising mineral in north Devon is anthracite coal. Although it has been mined in a very small localised way for fuel, in Bideford an associated clay-like substance was exploited for its carbon content for paint. The works was closed in 1970, after 46 years, and stripped, and the two inclined adits blasted shut. An electric winder hauled wagons out of the adits, one of which was accessed via an extremely tight 180° curve. June 1970.

OPPOSITE

Holman's Test Mine, Troon, Cornwall
SX 657368 Gauge 2ft
Not a proper mine, nor yet a quarry, Holman Bros maintained a test mine near Troon from the late 1930s to test and demonstrate their products and train apprentices. A 24-inch gauge tramway ran through the 7,000 feet of tunnels and mainly carried barren rock to the waste dumps. The pattern on the rock face to the left of the level entrance are test borings. May 1969

Quarrying

A great variety of rocks were quarried all over the south west; granite, limestone, sandstone, elvan, slate. Again a rail system was the ideal way of handling a heavy bulky material whether it was blocks of monumental stone or crushed roadstone. A simple layout sufficed for the former, often just a single line, of broad-ish gauge, from the working face to the dressing area, and another line to the dumps of waste rock. Slate quarry railways in the south west were not as developed as in north Wales but, like those in that area, were quite distinctive with specialised wagons. Roadstone quarrying flourished in the first half of the twentieth century, paving the way - perhaps literally - for the road transport revolution that was to sweep away many railways. They made use of Robert Hudson's products, and of similar manufacturers. The typically longer working face of such quarries was served by a fan of tracks, but after the second world war the rubber tyred dumper and the conveyor belt took over.

OPPOSITE: Bought new in 1901 when the railway opened, this 0-4-0WT was supplied through an agent, Arthur Koppel, hence it became known as *Koppel*. In the Great War this was changed to *Penlee*. It is now preserved at the Leighton Buzzard Light Railway, in Bedfordshire, where it has been cosmetically restored.

Penlee Quarry, Newlyn, Cornwall
SW 467281 Gauge 2ft

Gwavas Quarry really developed after the south pier of Newlyn Harbour was opened in 1885-6. It produced a very hard blue elvan rock, ideal for road building and many thousands of tons were shipped away until closure in 1992. Penlee is actually the name of an older quarry further south,

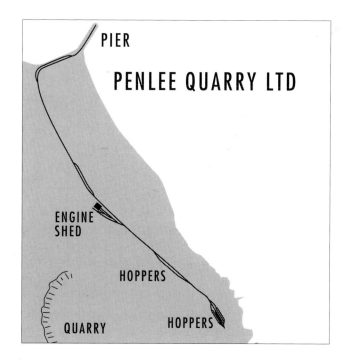

A loaded train waits to tip into the *MV Londonsbrooke* while the empties of the previous train are propelled back from the unloading tip on the South Pier at Newlyn. October 1962

near Mousehole, but the name was retained when operations moved north to Gwavas Quarry.

The railways was opened in 1901 when an 0-4-0 well tank was obtained from Germany, from builders Freudenstein. Increasing demand in the twenties and thirties saw numerous diesels acquired and the track was tripled in places by the mid-1930s. It remained busy until replaced by a conveyor in 1972. When a ship was in Newlyn Harbour trains of trucks shuttled continuously between hoppers and the pier, filling a ship between tides at the rate of 300 tons an hour.

Penlee brings a train onto the South Pier. 1938

Drawing wagons out of the hoppers in 1938. Comparison can be made with the 1961 view on page 32.

1954-built Ruston, named *J. W. Jenkin*, passes the line's original motive power. 1962

J. W. Jenkin, named after the head clerk of the quarry, RH 375315, pulls a loaded train away from the hoppers. 1961

Line-up at the hoppers after a day's working; Ruston Hornsbys 375316, 375315, 200748 and 287664. 1965

Ruston Hornsby 229656 shunting at the southern end of the hoppers, drawing empty wagons through and placing them for filling. October 1965

Empties were propelled back to the hoppers and problems could arise where lorries crossed the tracks. I took the precaution of asking if I could photograph the scene and was told not to tell the boss! October 1965

Rosenython Quarry, St. Keverne, Cornwall
SW 810215 Gauge 2ft

Part of Amalgamated Roadstone Corporation, the layout at Rosenython was simple and short, transferring stone from hoppers to either ships or lorries. It closed by 1979. Across the bay can seen the piers of Porthallow & Porthoustock Quarries. August 1977

Porthallow & Porthoustock Quarries, St Keverne, Cornwall
SX 808219 Gauge 2ft

Quarrying started here in the nineteenth century but was modernised in 1934. The line ran about a mile around the coast from Porthallow Quarry and up an incline to reach the hoppers and pier in Porthoustock . Work ceased in the late 1950s. September 1969

Kilmar Railway, Cornwall
Gauge 4ft 8¹/₂in

Built by the Cheesewring Granite Company in 1858 as a standard gauge extension of the Liskeard & Caradon Railway from Minions to their granite setts high on Bodmin Moor. The entire line of railway is above the 1,000 feet contour. Most of it fell out of use by the 1890s but its route of granite sleeper blocks survives as an excellent walk across the moor to Kilmar Tor.

Silver Grey Granite, Caradon Hill, Cornwall
SX 269075 Gauges 3ft & 3ft 6in

Typical of the heavily built wagons of a monumental stone quarry, this one was designed to carry massive pieces of granite from the quarry to the dressing sheds on the flanks of Caradon Hill. It was 3ft 6inch gauge but the other line which carried waste rock was 3ft. There were just the two lines. September 1967

Halwell Quarry, Coads Green, Cornwall
SX 305771 Gauge 17¹/₂in
The quarry was worked from 1920 to 1957 for ochre but in a very small way. The tramway ran on a substantial embankment in a straight line for over a third of a mile from the quarry to a loading bank on the road. Although well overgrown the rails were still on position and revealed a gauge of 17¹/₂ inches. May 1968

Old Delabole Slate Quarry, Delabole, Cornwall
SX 075835 Gauge 2ft
An amalgam of several old quarries in the early nineteenth century, Old Delabole had a rail system from about the middle of that century. It is said to have had a number of steam engines at one time as well as several impressive inclines powered by a Wadebridge built beam engine. Latterly a two-feet gauge powered incline brought slabs of slate out of the pit for dressing and splitting, with further tramways to the storage areas and waste dumps. June 1970.

Motor Rail 3739 of 1925 with a slab wagon, for carrying large pieces of uncut slate. 1968

A dumb buffered wagon used for carrying slit slates, quite different from those used in the Welsh slate quarries. 1968

Michaelstow Quarry, Cornwall
SX 088790 Gauge 2ft

Whilst many roadstone quarries were close to the sea, facilitating shipment, Cornwall County Council had several inland for their own use. Michaelstow was disused when I found it but appeared to have been worked by hand with very little mechanisation. Fans of tracks reached the working faces and converged to run back to the crusher and tar plant. April 1969

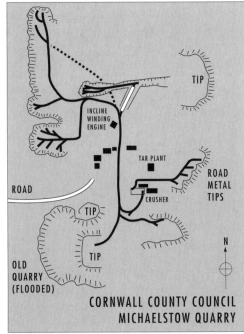

Tinhay Quarry, Lifton, Devon
SX 395851

East of Lifton village, close to the GWR station, the old A30 trunk road was flanked by two stone piers which, to anybody aware of Brunel's work in Cornwall, were obviously viaduct piers. I was aware of them long before I knew what an industrial railway was and speculated on the mysterious unrecorded railway that they must have carried. In fact they took waste stone from Tinhay Quarry to dumps on the south side of the GWR Launceston branch, which was crossed by an arch. A limekiln remains but the piers and arch have gone, and the trunk road now takes a less interesting route. February 1968

Lundy Granite Company, Lundy Island, Bristol Channel
SS 139450

For a few years in the 1860s the Lundy Granite Company exploited granite on the east side of Lundy Island, in the Bristol Channel. Now taken over by wildlife, the quarries remain and the routes of the tramways linking them with the dressing area can be clearly seen. An incline or slide took the stone down to ships in the bay below. 1978

Haytor Granite Tramway, Devon

One of the most remarkable railways of the South West, and almost unique in the British Isles, the Haytor Granite Tramway was built of the material it carried. Extending for some seven miles from the quarries at Haytor, on Dartmoor, to the Stover Canal, the rails were carved out of granite blocks, with a gauge of about 4ft 3ins. It opened in 1820 and was disused by 1858. The granite rails, having no scrap value, remain and its many branches, reaching into the quarries north of Haytor Rocks, can be explored.

Clay Extraction

The headings of mining or quarrying could have accommodated clay, since it is extracted by both methods, but clay extraction is important enough in the south west to justify its own heading.

China clay and ball clay are the principal products, and china stone is also included here. There was some brick clay extractions but I recorded very little of these.

China clay is washed out of pits using high pressure jets (monitors) and pumped away for processing. Narrow gauge tramways took away the waste, often on immense inclines. After settling the clay was trammed, on temporary tracks, from tanks into the drying kilns. The dried product was then transferred direct into main line railway wagons or, occasionally, by narrow gauge tramway to wagon or ship.

China stone was hard and quarried like stone and railed to crushing mills. Ground down with water it could then be pumped to dries whence it had the same treatment as china clay.

Ball clay was quite different, being of the texture we associate with clay. All production is now from open cast pits but formerly it was quarried or mined. In north Devon and Dorset not only was it taken from the pits by rail but it travelled on from the works by narrow gauge railway to either a shipping point or the main line railway, Dorset's first railway, Benjamin Fayle's Middlebere Plateway, opened in 1806 for this purpose.

Wheal Martyn. May 1975.

Pan Kiln Traverser (and settling tank)

Although rail systems were used in the pits to remove waste, china clay itself was not railed until 'settled' in tanks where the water content drained and evaporated off. It could then be dug out of the settling tanks using wagons on temporary tracks to transfer it into the pan kiln for heated drying. Below is a wagon on a travelling bridge, or traverser, which spanned the pan kiln and enabled the clay to be spread down the pan, thicker at the end near the furnace and thinner at the chimney end where the heat was less. This clay at Wenford Dry has been through a filter-press, which literally squeezed water out of it, and its appearance is a little different. After drying clay was shovelled into the linhay alongside and below. Gauges were usually 24-inch or 28-inch.

Examples of clay railways and wagons at Wheal Martyn China Clay Museum. On the left a wagon on typical temporary track that was laid into a settling tank. The clay would be carried through the door in the distance into the dry behind, straight onto the travelling bridge to be spread down the pan. (May 1975) Above is a reconstruction of the foot of an incline that would be used to extract waste from the pits to be dumped. (March 1978).

Carlyon Farm Dry, near St Austell, Cornwall
SX 013535 Gauges 2ft and 2ft 4in

Most pan kilns, or 'dries', lay alongside a main line siding and clay was simply transferred from the linhay into main line wagons. Carlyon Farm was built in 1919, alongside the GWR's new Trenance Valley branch, and was probably the largest dry in Cornwall. To maximise storage the linhay was very deep and short narrow gauge tracks recessed into the floor took the clay out onto centre pivotted drawbridges for tipping into main line wagons. The furnace was located centrally, with a chimney at each end of the dry. The tracks on one side were 24-inch gauge and the other 28-inch. The kiln was out of use by the time these photographs were taken in 1968.

Restowrack Quarry, Cornwall

OPPOSITE: The intricate network of lines serving the faces of this china stone quarry shows well. Some quarries used inclines to lift the stone to surface but Restowrack used cableways.

Two typical wagons in a typical clay district landscape. The wagon bodies pivotted and tipped. July 1966

Note the single bladed points on this primitive railway. 1979

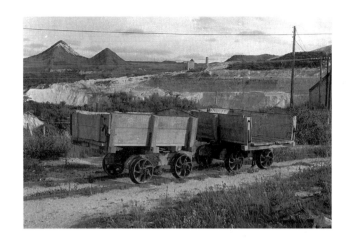

Tregargus Quarry, St Stephen, Cornwall
SW 949540 Gauge 2ft

A fascinating site that, after a hundred years work, fell out of use in the 1950s but was still intact the following decade. The quarry provided china stone to five water powered grinding mills, all linked by an intricate network of tramways and leats. There were five inclines and half a mile of 24-inch gauge track. May 1968.

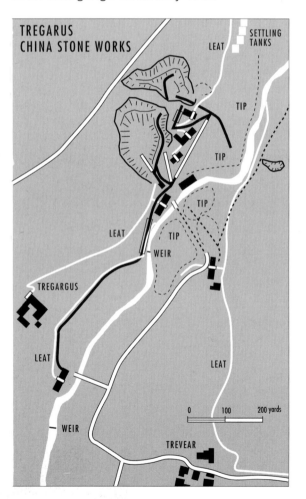

English China Clays, Ponts Mill, St Blazey, Cornwall
SX 072562 Gauge 4ft 8¹/₂in
An interesting relic was still in use at Ponts Mill. Rebuilt with a diesel engine, Motor Rail 2032 was originally built with petrol power in 1920. Ponts Mill was a remnant of the old Treffry's Tramways and although the site has been cleared there is much to see in this area. October 1962

English China Clays, Charlestown Dry, Charlestown, Cornwall
SX 039519 Gauge 2ft 4in
A new china clay dry was built at Charlestown in 1908 to ship clay via the tiny harbour there. The linhays were of hopper form, cut into the rock, and below in a tunnel ran a 28-inch gauge tramway which emerged high above the waiting ships. Another higher level line from the later dry served a lorry tip, now part of the shipwreck museum. 1968

The low bridge under the GWR main line. October 1967

Port of Par, Par Harbour, Cornwall

SX 076532 Gauge 4ft 8¹/₂in

ECC acquired the port of Par in 1964 having leased it since 1946. Some very odd standard gauge locomotives worked the harbour in early days but latterly a pair of Bagnall 0-4-0STs had the job. Due to a low bridge they had distinctively low cabs. Both *Judy* and *Alfred* are now preserved.

OPPOSITE: *Alfred* on shed. September 1964

Lee Moor Tramway, Devon
Gauge 4ft 6in

A remarkable line inherited by ECC, along with Lee Moor clay works in 1919. The LMT was opened in 1856 to give the clay pits at Torycombe, at one time the largest in the world, access to the sea at Cattewater. It acquired its gauge of 4ft 6inches from the Plymouth & Dartmoor Railway (opened 1823) which it branched from. Being the older line LMT trains had precedence on its level crossing of the GWR main line at Laira. The section between the two cable operated inclines was steam operated and after closure in 1960 both locomotives were preserved.

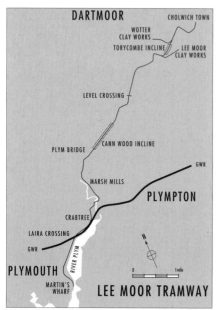

The late Roy Taylor, author of *The Lee Moor Tramway*, who played a leading part in the restoration, stands proudly beside *Lee Moor No 2* (Peckett 784 of 1899) outside the shed at Torycombe. April 1968.

OPPOSITE: (above) The overgrown passing loop on the Cann Wood incline. June 1961
(below) Contractors are busy lifting the line but their lorry seems to have broken down. The signal was to protect Whitegates Crossing. June 1961

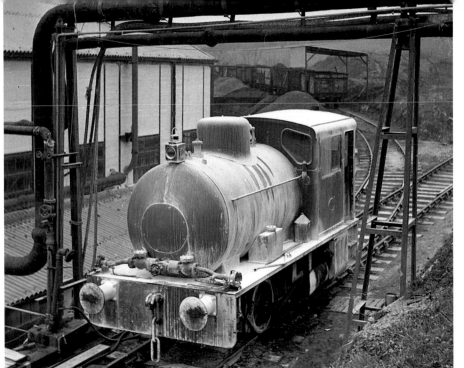

English China Clays, Marsh Mills, Plymouth, Devon

SX 523577 Gauge 4ft 8¹⁄₂in

In a few places ECLP sidings were extensive enough to need their own locomotive power. At Marsh Mills was a fireless loco, fairly rare in the south west. This was filled with boiling water from a stationary source and under pressure the steam powered the locomotive for some time. It was Bagnall 3121 of 1957 and dumped out of use was the diesel it replaced, Fowler 22917 of 1940. March 1962

Redlake Tramway, Ivybridge, Devon
Gauge 3ft

Engineered by R Handsford Worth and opened by the China Clay Corporation in 1911, the Redlake Tramway ran for some seven miles into Dartmoor from clays dries alongside the GWR main line near Ivybridge. Several quite interesting locomotives were used until closure in 1933 and now the route makes a useful path into the moor.

The engine shed stands on the edge of the moor beyond the head of the incline that dropped the line to the clay dries.

Seen here about to leave Redlake with one of the workmen's carriages, *Dartmoor* was an 0-4-2 saddle tank built by Kerr Stuart in 1911.

North Devon Clay Co Ltd., Peters Marland, Devon

SS 504125 Gauges 3ft & 4ft 8½in

The North Devon Clay system, although extensive enough, was the remains of a much longer line. The ball clay workings were restarted on a business like scale in the 1870s and to connect with the L&SWR main line at Torrington the Torrington & Marland Railway was built. The engineer was the noted John Barraclough Fell and he chose three feet gauge. When this line was superceded by the standard gauge North Devon & Cornwall Light Railway, engineered by another famous name, Holman Fred Stephens, in 1925, the system just connected the pits and the mines to the works and the NDCJLR siding. From that time the works also had its own standard gauge locomotive. Diesels worked from the late 1940s but the narrow gauge system succumbed to road in 1970. The standard gauge lasted until closure of the BR line in 1982.

A feature of the T&MR were the timber viaducts designed by Fell to span rivers and valleys. *Mary* crosses the Torridge Viaduct with a train that includes the two ex-London horse trams bought for workmen's transport.

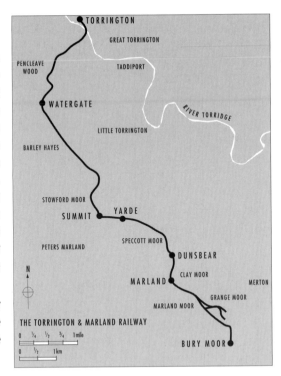

THE TORRINGTON & MARLAND RAILWAY

The three Fletcher Jennings 0-4-0STs bought second-hand in 1908 were too heavy for the light track around the pits and works so, in this case, the saddle tank was removed to a separate tender. Two good locos were rebuilt out of the three and they lasted until the late forties, at least.

Surviving in 1968 was the former tender of one of the Fletcher Jennings locos.

At least three of the sturdy open wagons were converted in vans, with wooden seats around their perimeter, for carrying workmen and these lasted to the end of the railway's life. May 1968

Progress was John Fowler's first 400 class 60hp diesel built in 1945 and given the works number 4000001. It was bought new for the clay works and, being the first diesel at Marland, was appropriately named. It was rebuilt at the works in 1977 with a hydraulic transmission replacing the original three-speed gearbox. May 1968

Ruston Hornsby 446207 of 1961 brings a train of clay into the works area. To the right of the train is the narrow gauge engine shed with the main works building to the right of that. The lines on the right are standard gauge and *Progress* can be seen in the disance. May 1968

The clay moors of Petrockstow were fairly bleak, even on a fine day, and these three views, all taken in May 1968 give a good impression of the wilderness that surrounded the mines. The mine heads were flimsy ramshackle affairs, loosely clad in corrugated iron sheeting and reflecting their ephemeral nature. The shafts were steeply inclined and the skip tipped directly into the three feet gauge wagons. A narrower gauge line was often used to take unusable waste clay to one side.

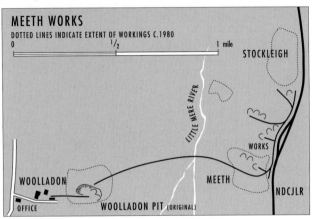

MEETH WORKS
DOTTED LINES INDICATE EXTENT OF WORKINGS C.1980
0   ½   1 mile

STOCKLEIGH

LITTLE MERE RIVER

WORKS

WOOLLADON

MEETH

NDCJLR

OFFICE

WOOLLADON PIT (ORIGINAL)

Standard two-foot gauge side-tip wagons were used but modified with timber bodies to prevent the clay being stained by rust. May 1968

Meeth (North Devon) Clay Co Ltd, Meeth, Devon
SS 538086 Gauge 2ft
The ball clay pits at Meeth were established in 1920 when the approaching NDCJLR made transport from the Meeth basin viable. Rail working ceased soon after the ECC take-over in 1965 and all working became opencast by 1970.

A clear indication of the softness of the ground is the use of former standard gauge sleepers to support two-foot gauge track. Beyond is one of the shallow inclined shafts. May 1968

The ubiquitous Ruston diesel was the motive power at Meeth, although at an earlier time two Fordson tractor conversions by Muir Hill were used. This Ruston is 237897 of 1945, not seeing a lot of use. May 1968

Furzebrook, Dorset

The ball clay deposits of the Isle of Purbeck gave rise to several industrial railways shown on the map. The central line is Fayle's Tramway, a plateway of 3ft 9inches gauge, opened in 1806 to Middlebere. To the north from 1840 a 2ft 8inch gauge tramway ran to Ridge and the line to the south is the 3ft 9inch Goathorn Tramway which replaced an earlier plateway running inland from the pier of that name. The lines that survived were regauged to two-foot in 1948 and closed in 1972.

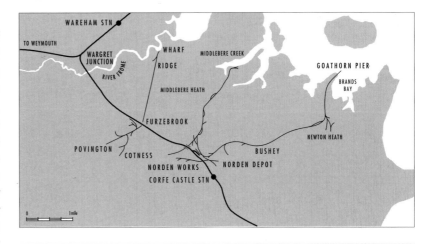

OPPOSITE: On the two-foot gauge of Pike Bros, Fayle & Co., a Ruston diesel spends the weekend in one of the clay sheds at Eldon Siding, near Corfe Castle, on the Swanage branch. 1967

All the timeless atmosphere of a rural industrial railway, as a 1936 Ruston, 175413, brings two wagons up from the mines towards Eldon Siding. 1964.

As a change from the usual Rustons Fayle & Co bought a couple of second-hand 1930's Orenstein & Koppel 35hp 0-4-0 diesel mechanical locos and these survived derelict to be preserved in 1972.

Alongside the track leading to the mines, on the left, is the cab back-plate of *Tiny*, a Lewin 0-4-0ST of 1868 that ran on the 3 feet 9 inch gauge line from Norden to Goathorn. The line was converted to 1ft 11½inch gauge in 1948 and *Tiny* was scrapped. For a period after 1948 this line also saw *Russell* from the Welsh Highland Railway used, but that locomotive was rescued for preservation and now is running again in Snowdonia. 1968

Shallow inclined shafts were used in Purbeck and this view is looking towards the shaft with the winding house behind the camera. Note the winding cable and the small tub wagons. 1968

OPPOSITE: The tub wagons were drawn along to a shed where they could be tipped into wagons on the wider gauge railway or, latterly, into road vehicles.

Other Industries

A great variety of other industries used industrial railways. Gas works often had their coal supplies delivered by rail and by-products taken the same way so needed to manoeuver full wagons around the site. Docks had need to move heavy machinery and their supplies, too, often came in by rail. The peat beds of the Somerset levels were too soft to permit road vehicles so light two-foot gauge tracks spread like tentacles across the peat moors. Just as contractors had used industrial railways to build Britain's main line railway network so their successors, the scrapping contractors, used them to dismantle the network.

OPPOSITE: The earliest locomotives used here were built by the local Penryn engineering firm of Sara & Burgess, who built at least half a dozen similar vertical boilered engines, included the GWR 0-4-0 *Tiny*, now preserved as the only surviving original broad gauge locomotive. This is one of the Falmouth engines, apparently before 1892 and conversion to standard gauge.

In 1926 Falmouth Docks purchased three new Hawthorn Leslie 0-4-0ST locomotives, and a fourth in 1927, spelling the end for the Sara & Burgess engines. No 3 was originally No1 but numbers were swapped for some reason in 1955. Note the spark arrester on the chimney. 1964

Falmouth Dock & Engineering Co Ltd, Falmouth, Cornwall
SW 822324 Gauge 4ft 8¹/₂in
One of the few 'heavy' industries on the south west, Falmouth Docks were established in 1859 and had a broad gauge rail connection as soon as the Cornwall Railway reached Falmouth in 1863. It was re-gauged to standard in 1892. Steam remained here until quite late as such power was of more use in helping manouevre ships in and out of docks.

On 4 July 1964 the Plymouth Railway Circle arranged a formal visit to the docks and its railway and one result was this line-up of 0-4-0STs. Heading the row is No 5, a Hudswell Clarke of 1929, followed by No 4 (Hawthorn Leslie 1927), No 3 (Hawthorn Leslie 1926) and No 6 (Peckett 1929).

OPPOSITE: No 6 was a Peckett built in 1919 and bought second-hand in 1961. 1963

The docks also had a remarkably interesting collection of rolling stock for internal purposes. This four-wheel wooden side-tipping wagon was probably quite ancient and survived to be photographed in 1959.

Wagon No 106 is of wooden construction with dumb buffers. The steam crane behind is one of many that worked all around the dock area. 1964

OPPOSITE: Many of the internal wagons came from main line companies. Van No 6 is ex-LNER and other vehicles came from the Caledonian Railway and the Great Eastern. 1964

Pentewan Sands, Pentewan, Cornwall

SX 020472 Gauge 2ft 6in

Pentewan Harbour was the terminus of the Pentewan Railway, opened privately in 1829 on about 4 foot gauge, and converted to 2ft 6 inch in 1872 when steam was introduced. It primarily served the china clay industry but closed in 1917. A new industrial railway was soon in place at the harbour serving the concrete block works and bringing sand from the beach. This kept the same gauge as some Pentewan Railway wagons were retained for its use but there was little other connection with the former system. Although mainly intact, with the Ruston Hornsby locomotives locked in the shed, the system was out of use when I first saw it in 1961.

Very substantial Hudson side-tip wagons were in use, of 3 feet wheelbase and with 19 inch diameter wheels. August 1961

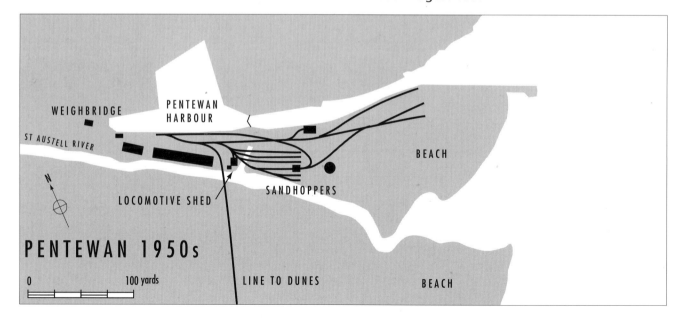

WEIGHBRIDGE

PENTEWAN HARBOUR

ST AUSTELL RIVER

LOCOMOTIVE SHED

SANDHOPPERS

BEACH

N

PENTEWAN 1950s

0   100 yards

LINE TO DUNES

BEACH

Looking north in 1968, a glimpse of the former layout can be seen amongst the remains. The concrete viaduct on the edge of the harbour was a successor to the Pentewan Railway timber one for loading ships. February 1968

St Michael's Mount, Cornwall
SW 515300 Gauge 2ft 5¹/₂in

One line which survives and remains in use on a regular basis transports goods from the harbour on the Mount up to the castle. It is 2ft 5¹/₂in gauge, about 650 feet long and rises 173 feet, most of the way in a tunnel. It is cable operated and has just one wagon. 1969

William Hodge's Limekiln, Moorswater, Cornwall
SX 236642 Gauge 2ft 6in

A remarkable survival is a plateway turntable on top of this limekiln. The kiln was built by William Hodge in 1830 and limestone was hauled up an inclined plateway from the canal basin beneath. Haulage was by a waterwheel powered winch and remains of the waterwheel and the winch survive as well as the turntable. In this photograph a young sapling has pushed the turntable up out of its base. 1972.

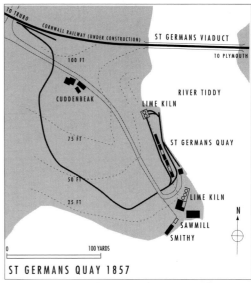

ST GERMANS QUAY 1857

St Germans Quay Tramway, Cornwall
SW 960556

One of the more unusual lines in Cornwall was a short, and short-lived, tramway built by the contractors building the Cornwall Railway about 1859. It was very steep and dropped from St Germans station down to the Quay in order to gain access to the sea for bringing materials in. Little trace now remains of the route but the ledge running to the top of the limekilns is quite clear.

Bude Canal Tramway, Bude Cornwall
SS 205064 Gauge 2ft

Another line that carried sand was that at Bude. As early as 1825 a plateway of 4ft gauge was laid onto the beach to bring sand to the canal basin to load boats. It was used for agricultural purposes. About 1920 it was replaced with a 2ft gauge line, along which the people nearest the camera are walking. June 1978

South Western Gas Board, Devon
With coal to move in and coke and by-products to move out, gas works were ideal sites for industrial railways, forming the link between the works and the main line railway.

OPPOSITE: Exeter gas works (SX 921918) in the 1960s had two steam locomotives built by Peckett of Bristol. One of them, 2074 of 1946, is seen here shunting. April 1962

Torquay's Hollacombe Gas Works (SX 898622) more modestly had a Ruston Hornsby 48 h.p. diesel, 402809 of 1956, a class 48DS, but the view was much better. July 1967

United Dairies, Chard Junction, Somerset

ST 341047 Gauge 4ft 8¹/₂in

With the growth of main line railways and their ability to transfer dairy products rapidly and freshly to the major cities, milk production became an important industry in the south west. Only at Chard Junction was there an industrial locomotive to shunt the siding there. This is a 44 h.p. Ruston Hornsby diesel of 1937, no 183062. June 1965

Exeter Corporation Sewage Works, Devon

Gauge 2ft

An unexpected photograph. Colin Shears, of the West of England Transport Collection at Winkleigh, had bought a Motor Rail petrol locomotive and five wagons from Exeter Sewage Works. Having picked them up on one of his vintage lorries he brought the whole load to the Umberleigh Traction Engine Rally, which I had called in on my way back from visiting the clay works at Petrockstow and Meeth. May 1968

Railway Contractors

Industrial railways and locomotives were, inevitably, used in the construction of main line and branch line railways. Rather less welcome was their use in dismantling such lines after closure.

Pittrail Ltd had the contract for lifting the Chacewater - Newquay branch and used a Barclay 0-6-0 diesel 336 of 1939. This diesel, seen here at Perranporth, is older than many steam engines in this book. March 1964

An unknown contractor was using a 1940 Fowler 0-4-0 diesel (22920) at Lyme Regis. It was marked 'Risley Yd. No 111 MED', indicating its former (military) ownership. May 1967

British Railways

The main line railway companies have always maintained locomotives, rolling stock and track for their own internal purposes and these are technically industrial railways too.

At Broad Clyst (SX 992953) the Southern Railway, and later BR, maintained a sleeper depot and to shunt the siding here they kept Ruston Hornsby 237923, a class 48DS diesel of 1946. July 1964

Exmouth Junction motive power depot (SX 940958) had a very crude internal works tramway of 19in gauge, probably installed when the depot was built in 1927. It ran around two sides of the building and had no points, as all junctions were at right angles with turning plates. Basic four wheel trolleys were used to move heavy objects about. The depot closed in 1970. 1965

Meldon Quarry (SX 568928), near Okehampton, was worked by locomotives transferred from capital stock. My visits were at weekends when nothing was working and the resident engine was un-photograhically parked in its shed. In 1962 the resident was ex-LSWR 0-6-0T of 1898, numbered DS682 but the following year its place had been taken by an ex-USA 0-6-0T, DS234. This had been built by Vulcan Iron Works, of Philadelphia, in 1942 for war service and a number later found their way into the hands of the Southern Railway.

Sidmouth Harbour Tramway, Devon

SY 121869 Gauge 3ft 8in

In 1836 a scheme was started to build a harbour at the west end of Sidmouth beach. Stone was to come from beyond the east end and a wooden railway was built to carry it, partially in a tunnel in the cliffs to protect the line from storms. A steam locomotive, possibly the first in Devon, was bought from Neath Abbey Ironworks in south Wales but proved too big for the tunnel. Despite a grand ceremony when the foundation stone was laid nothing more was done and Sidmouth still has no harbour. Part of the wooden track, carried on piles,

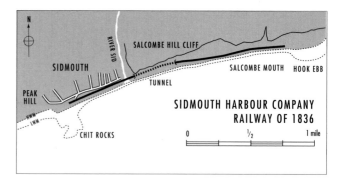

buried by cliff falls, was uncovered in 1967 but removed by sea before a section could be salvaged.

Eclipse Peat Co, Ashcott, Somerset

ST 454406 Gauge 2ft

Another terrain that, like the clay basins, suited rail was the peat beds of the Somerset levels. The high water table kept the ground very soft and it was the lowering of this that spelt the end of the several industrial railways, as well as causing adverse effects on the natural environment. These photographs were taken on an RCTS visit in October 1965; normally the peat workings were much lonelier places.

The main peat beds, Great Plains, were separated from Broomfield Works by a public road and, alas, narrow gauge trains were not able to cross the road, although the grooves in the road suggested that they did from time to time. Laden peat wagons were hauled up this loading ramp to be tipped into road vehicles for the final part of the journey across the road to the works.

Broomfield works sported this three way point at the entrance to the mill. The workshop was to the right.

Lightly laid track running across the peat beds.

OPPOSITE: A typical train on the Somerset peat railways. A small Lister locomotive (26366 of 1944) and three peat wagons. Behind can be seen the stacks of cut peat drying off.

Several of the Listers sported canopies to give the driver some protection from the elements, as on 34758 of 1949 here.

Even less sophisticated was this locomotive, made by the works themselves. A 32hp Lister diesel engine was mounted on a wagon chassis.

OPPOSITE: Remarkably the peat lines crossed the former Somerset & Dorset Railway's Highbridge branch. An accident here in earlier years had put a standard gauge locomotive in the ditch.

A few non-Lister engines were at Ashcott. Motor Rail Simplex 4604 of 1932 went to the scrapman the year after our visit. The round tank on the left is the cooling system for the engine.

In the shed at Ashcott was this venerable Muir Hill, A125 of 1925. Muir Hill made a chassis into which a Fordson tractor engine and transmission was dropped, the wheels being driven by a chain under the protective housing seen on the right hand side of the loco. This too was scrapped in 1966.

Trinity House, North Light, Lundy Island, Bristol Channel

SS 131481 Gauge 2ft

Possibly the most difficult railway in the south west to reach, this short two foot gauge line took supplies brought by sea for the lighthouse at the northernmost tip of Lundy Island. Goods were hauled up a cableway from the Trinity House tender and transferred to the railway to run down to the lighthouse. Automation of lighthouses and the installation of helicopter pads has since made it redundant. 1978

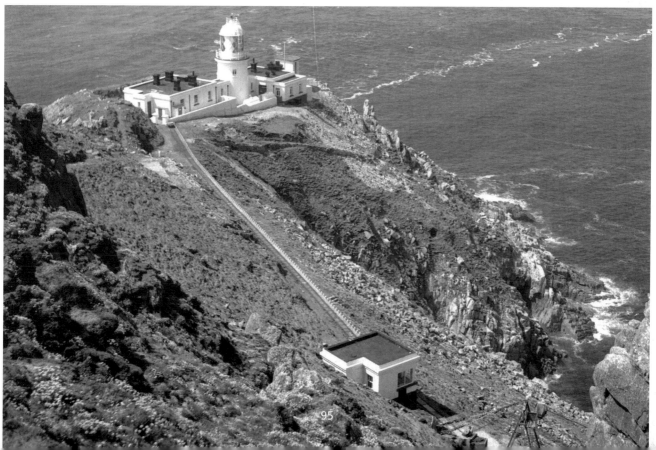

Bibliography

Books:

Barton, D. B. *The Redruth & Chasewater Railway*, Barton 1966

Brooks, Tony. *Great Rock - Devon's Last Metal Mine,* Cornish Hillside 2004

Ewans, M. C. *The Haytor Granite Tramway and Stover Canal*, David & Charles 1964

Fairclough, T & Shepherd, E *Mineral Railways of the West Country*, Barton 1975

Hateley, Roger (compiler) *Industrial Locomotives of South Western England*, Industrial Railway Society 1977

Lewis, M. J. T. *The Pentewan Railway*, Twelveheads Press 1981

Messenger, Michael J. *North Devon Clay*, Twelveheads Press 1982

Messenger, Michael J. *Caradon & Looe; the Canal. Railways and Mines*, Twelveheads Press 2001

Oeyenhausen & Dechen *Railways in England 1826 and 1827*, Newcomen Society 1971

Stanier, Peter. *Quarries of England & Wales,* Twelveheads Press 1995

Taylor, R. E. *The Lee Moor Tramway*, Twelveheads Press 1999

Wade, E. A. *The Redlake Tramway*, Twelveheads Press 2004

Articles:

Farmer, Keith. - Amalgamated Roadstone, *Industrial Railway Record* 1968

Legg, Chris. - The Middlebere Plateway, *Swanage Railway Magazine* Autumn 2000

Messenger, Michael J. - Sidmouth Harbour Company of 1836, *Industrial Railway Record* 1974

Messenger, Michael J. - Early Cornish Mineral Railways, *Jno of the Railway & Canal Historical Society* 1976

Messenger, Michael J. - Bulkamore Iron Mine, *Industrial Railway Record* 1977

Messenger, Michael J. - Early Cornish Mineral Railways, *Jno of the Trevithick Society* 1978

Messenger, Michael J. - The St Germans Tramway, *Industrial Railway Record* 1993

Moon, George. - Norden, Eldon's Siding and the Middlebere Plateway, *Swanage Railway Magazine* Summer 2000

Moseley, Brian - Railway to Rattlebrook, *Devon Life* April 1977

Semmens, P.W.B. - St Michael's Mount Tramway, *Railway Magazine* 1964

Smith-Grogan, G. - The Tramways of West Penwith, *Industrial Railway Record* 1991